SEIZE

Also by Brian Komei Dempster

Topaz

SEIZE

Brian Komei Dempster

To Sawala,

With admiration and respect for your beautiful artistry and spirit. So glad we had the chance to meet.

Brian Kei Dew

June 20, 2023

Four Way Books

Tribeca

for Brendan, my brave son

Library of Congress Cataloging-in-Publication Data

Names: Dempster, Brian Komei, [date]- author.
Title: Seize / poems by Brian Komei Dempster.
Description: New York : Four Way Books, [2020] |
Series: A Stahlecker series selection |
Identifiers: LCCN 2019054708 | ISBN 9781945588518 (trade paperback)
Subjects: LCGFT: Poetry.
Classification: LCC PS3604.E4755 S45 2020 | DDC 811/.6--dc23
LC record available at https://lccn.loc.gov/2019054708

This book is manufactured in the United States of America and printed on
acid-free paper.

Four Way Books is a not-for-profit literary press. We are grateful for the assistance
we receive from individual donors, public arts agencies, and private foundations.

This publication is made possible with public funds from the
New York State Council on the Arts, a state agency.

We are a proud member of the Community of Literary Magazines and Presses.

Contents

Night Sky 3

Notes

Night Sky

At his birth, I held my son against stars,
charted the climb, his flag among stars.

A jagged pulse shook our space—
his mind, a blizzard of stars.

I keep it quiet, how he sees earth
crooked, his words, buried stars.

———————   · · ·   ———————

Seize

Blue flame
                in the eye's corner,
stove on
        high, we brace
                for his flint
        and spark, our dark
surprise, his smile
                jolts, head
        unleashed, little body
                        arched, straining
                in the high
chair, we stand
                to face
        anything, she steadies
                his tray, eggs bubble
        in the pot, I lunge
                for his spoon, his purple
elephant, water boils
                over sides, we look
        to each other, sense
the sizzle, his bowl
        clattering, a reverse
                        crater, we shake off
                faults, shells

7

crack, window

shut, we smell

the heat, hardened

yolks, his brain's singed

gray, the scorched

black dome,

we are all

hollowed out.

A Boy

We knocked Jake Brown
to the ground

in eighth grade, kept him there
with words, *Get up, retard*. A man

is born strong. *I dare*

you. A boy is meant to stand up.
But Jake wouldn't. My son Brendan

can't. Day after day. It hurts to see him
stuck. The report branded

him *retarded, abnormal, impaired,*

delayed. Waves of words. In water
I make him

new. Rub spasms
from his back. *Come on, Brendan.*

Help me. Flat on his belly, he hugs

the shower's tiled ground. *Please, son.* Tries to pull
himself up. Slips. Ripples

the white curtain. He's
safe. No blood

this time. Just clear streams

pearling. I keep
fit. Lift weights so I can lift

him. Kneeling, I raise him slow. *Why can't you
do this on your own?* Soap-slick bird,

my six-year-old boy slips

through my hands. *Can you
make things easier*

just this once? I hold
tighter, won't let

him slip

again. Jake's eyes crossed behind bifocals,
he'd fumbled

my pinpoint pass, tripped
at the rim. My boy stays smaller

than other boys. Still it hurts

to lower myself
to him. I need

more strength. Old words foam inside
me, held back. *Are you*

an idiot? My son looks

away, water streaks
his face, washes

away tears, his mouth
bitter with Dove suds, words

that never roll off

his tongue. *Sissy*. Jake lost us
the game. *You play*

like a girl. Behind the veil
our shadows. In steam I tell myself

words will dissolve, droplets

soothing my mouth, running down my chest
onto Brendan's back.

Four years ago, I told the doctor,
my voice measured, *Be careful*

with those words. The shower stream grows

cold, I am naked
and shivering. In the drain's dark well

our echoes. I want to believe
in him. It was just

a report. Jake's bifocals cracked,

he pissed
his Toughskins. *Moron.* More than

a word. Sprawled like Jake
on pavement, my son spreads out

his arms, little wings

spanning the damp
expanse. My feet sank

into wet grass. Jake ran from us,
sandy hair whipping

his freckles. *Sorry, Daddy*

didn't mean it.
Because he's my boy,

it's my fault. I need new
words. *Waking bird. Fierce*

starling. My hands pat him dry, smooth

his hair. It shines
like feathers. One skinny leg

kicks out.
His hands search

the wall,

push me away
to lift off alone,

stand up to me
just this once.

Seized

By day. By night. In handcuffs. Through mind-scramble. Brain-

surged. Shock of force, body taut. Alerted. Taken.

Outside. Inside. Anytime. Any place. No words to explain. My

infant mother, 1942. My young son now. The rug,

his twisted body, his world inside. And what it does. Red flare

or white lightning. Fried impulse or smoldering

heat. A searing of gray or glitter of stars veiled by fog. Her

fragments. Yellow orb, the porch light. Shimmer

against her face. The cradle, her mother's arms. A blanket's false

cover. Itch of wool, hives on skin. Things

just happen. By bus. By train. In war. Electric storms. A horse

stable. Desert. Sand swirl and mind gust. Thought

sparks. Word cloudings. Mountains spike against white. A guard's

boot. Trodden syllable. A thorned cage. Wing

pierced. Baby hawk in wire. My barbed string of words. To capture

him. Capture her. If he never speaks? I carry him. If

she cries for her father? Grandmother carries her. Some place. My mother

carries what is unremembered. Begins to know

when I ask. I don't speak. Of things I can't know. Of despair about

my son. We never know. Where we are going. Where

love will end us.

My Mother at One

I am the baby
      erased

from every war

      story. The wish
empty in Father's

      hands. Our cord torn

by razor
      wire, skies of violet

plasma. I sense

      boredom
in mosquitoes, the itch

      beneath skin. Fall asleep

to the rake
      of Topaz

wind, desert willows

bending over
the stone tablet

of earth. Nighttime

my body curled—
slashed by

the quarter

moon. Waves of heat
and waiting. My lips

on a bottle's nib,

sand in
the face, Mother

stooped over

stairs, always
rocking me.

Brendan's Key

An invisible cage—

>   we feel him

locked. His quiet

>   bangs against

us. He taps

>   our hands—right

yes, left *no*. Drops

>   the ring

of keys

>   at our feet, *Car ride now.*

His trail shadowed—

>   we follow clues. Thoughts

shining

>   through him. Coins.

Spoons. Falling,

>   clanging. We pick them

up. His heart

      a small jar

of lost things. A silver

      window. Light trapped,

he touches sun

      on glass. Closes

and opens

      a thousand

doors.

Brendan Lexicon

Angel, Lion,
      Bird. Cluster
seizures. He splashes,
      barks
in baths, screams
      near edges
of pools. Loves
      the school bus. Hates

Grace cutting
      his fingernails. Loves
and hates most
      things. On some
spectrum. Shrieking angel, palsied
      lion, intractable bird. Falls
in cracks between labels. My son. Nine years
      old. *Ma, hai, duh* his own

language. Atonic drops. Intermittent.
      He chases robins, flings
our clothes. Against chairs
      pounds tennis
balls. Claws tabletops
      for dishes, tosses

spoons, thumps his feet
       to funk

beats, dunks
       orange ball, body checks
the plastic hoop. Focal motor
       misfires. Disco bird. Point guard
lion. Wrecking
       angel. We clap
for simple
       things. Guide him back

when he misses
       the toilet, piss staining
his pants. Sit too
       close, he moves
away. Sit far away,
       he moves close. His sounds
fly by,
       he lets out

a sad roar through grinding
       teeth. Staring spells. Clonic shaking.
Night through skylights, our peaceful

time. Grace and I
on opposite couches. Flipping
          channels. Backs
stiff. Pulsing
          temples. Sleeping

through *Mad*
          Men. True Blood.
Waking
          to melted
coffee ice cream.
          It's not
that simple. To love
          him so much. To hate

just some of it.

The Door

If I am not perfect, everything falls apart. I steady
my epileptic son, pull the handle
of the front door. Stuck. Nowhere to go. Last night
I held Grace. Entered her. *Are you ready for another child?*
she asked. *It could help us.* Winter rain arrived, the night
damp and cold. We slept together for the first time

this week. Would the new child be normal? Protect or resent
Brendan? Marriage is our son, marriage is shutting him out.
Turning my back, I kneel down, free the mat under the door. I am
trying to get us somewhere. It slants open, a sliver
of light. My pulse quickens—where did
Brendan go? A crash behind me. His screams. I run

to find him—on the ground, his head bleeding. *What
are you doing?* I yell at him, at myself. *Calm down*
Grace says, *It's not his fault.* We are closed in. She holds
him tight. I reach a threshold, pull him back
to me. Could I have been there? She touches
my wrist. Can Grace and I get back

to us? I sleep alone, in the room next to his. Listening.
The strum of blinds. He'll stand up. Sway on his bed. I'll rush
in. Rain sweeps leaves from gutters. More nights

apart. Grace's warmth beyond reach. Her words to me
when he stopped crying, *I'm close to wanting
another.* My face against her hair, its apple scent,

my words shutting her out. *Not quite yet.* I am trying
to stay open.

Truce

Some days
     we are

bombed harbors,

          then silence.
Other days

          I speak, my voice

a snake, cursive
          in deserts. A father

and son. Two

          countries. Flags whipping
in wind. I know the words

          I need

               *

to whisper. Words
      keeping us

apart. My shirt twisted

      in his fist, he tugs
at me. Back turned, I shake him

      off. My torn

sleeve, a white cloth
      he holds up. Shots fire

from my mouth. *Stop. Tell me*

      what you want—
words in our own war story

      he can't

     *

answer. My son
        seized. Ancestors

trapped. Grandmother walks

        on boards, carries
my baby mother over mud and horse shit

        of Tanforan. Wraps her

with blankets in Topaz—their sand
        prison. Images

sizzle in his eyes. Light forking

        the sky, Mother
blinks. Like my son, she

        doesn't know

        *

the words. Bedtime
                stories, a nightly

clash, my hands guiding

                his head, forcing him
back to the page. Rain

                on tin, hum of songs, her father

missing. Empty deserts. Shudder
                of flags. The mouth and its silent

dust. Between quiet

                and the noise, I reach
the edge. Almost

                surrender.

Jap

after Bob Hicok

It shot out of Mr. Foster's mouth, I flinched while he took aim
     at *fucking kamikaze* crows

who dove from the sky, landed in rows of his prized tomatoes, bore
     into red and yellow flesh. It rode

the air, clipped me, an arrow dipped in blood from beaks, sharp

     and fast as gold beads
from his cocked rifle. Mixed with *Get out*, slurred

     by Budweiser chugs from cans
our neighbor Mr. F crumpled with his hands, flattened

     with his boot soles, it bubbled

in beer foam, softened by the paper bag of heirlooms
     Mr. F brought to our front

door. *The best ones . . . I picked them for you* he told
     my mother. His gift appeasing

the boundary between continents, our backyards, like the free advice

he offered my father as I stood
behind fence slats, listening: *Place old tires deep in soil*

　　　for ripe tomatoes. Scatter seeds
for crows. It was his gaze shifting sudden to a bird

　　　overhead, his liquored breath

and insistence at how sneaky *we* were, and *Why did you marry one?*
　　　he asked my father, *You better watch*

out. His raided garden of fallen globes. A failed crop. My mother Renko
　　　and father Stuart growing me—their heirloom—

too many shades of us for him, the enemy in me, her almond eyes

　　　and olive skin, crows lifting
off, Mr. F's drunken misses bringing him to his knees, his downed

　　　plane a half-century
ago, his claps and my gasps when they landed

backwards, black bellies

up. It cut through my father's nervous smile, *Hey buddy,*
     just don't say it . . .

Mr. F's reply *I won't say it around your wife . . .* I backed
     away from his bruised

harvest, furrowed trenches speckled with gunpowder, birds

     flapping wings
in dirt, Mr. F's barrel tarnished like his burning

     plane, sinking into the ocean
where he was stranded, shrapnel from his war embedded

     in parts of me.

Dissonance

The call reaching me first, my tires slide through turns,
      I want to kill, arrive

too late, find Loren, my younger brother, dazed

      at the bed's edge. Ripped packets
of smelling salts, ammonia shocks

      him awake, *What happened?*

Who did this to you? Where's the ambulance? I squeeze
      my fist, nails cutting

into my palm. *Where are they?*

      Don't my brother
says. The school nurse steadies

      his loose front tooth, sweeps her pen of light

over his bruised
      skin. *He'll be ok. He needs quiet.* I hold

a bag of ice against his face, his throat

     rasping, *Where's my music?* I replay
Loren's fragments: his shoulder, brushed

     against one of them, their eyes,

glared at him, he only knew Andre,
     who had picked him

for his team in gym class, *Sorry I didn't*

     see you, Loren's thoughts lost
in a Bach suite, *What'd you say?* the cleared

     hallway, *Get out the way*

white boy their faces closing
     in, his plea *I'm not*

white their flurry of fists, kicks,

     Andre's girlfriend, Tasha, says *Stop. Leave him*
alone Loren swings his right, saves the left

for the frets, he repeats *I'm half-Japanese*, no one

listening, only Jerome, who played violin
    with him, *Yeah man, he's like one*

of us Loren's cello case, a dented

    shield, screech of Converse, knocked down
to his knees, gold strings snap, whip

    inside. His body curled up,

they run. Tasha kneels
    close, *I'll stay.* Jerome springs up, *I'll go*

get help. My fingers numb, I set down the ice, cover

    my brother's skinned knuckles
with a damp cloth. *Mom and Dad*

    are almost here. Lights

burn, walls bend, on the floor
    his coat, backpack spilling

out, he sways, I brace

      him, our eyes on torn pages—notes
he blurs double.

Bandage

I wake
        between two worlds,

                resin bags split open, lockers

they slammed me against,
        and here, my safe bedroom,

                the quivering

air. I squint
        at my cello, expecting

                blows, reach for

my bow—cracked
        in half. Night unpeels, faces

                circle me, their eyes, jagged

stars. The beating rises,
        quiets. Shadows

of notes

on walls. Steel shudders, their
    retreat, the school's cold floor

        against my cheek. I climb

the ladder
    of frets, reach blurred

        passages. My head

echoes, missing
    beats, fingers

        tense, bandaged

bow hand resting. From
    a suite, three notes

        begin, vibrato, then silence, their feet

stilled in empty
        hallways.

Storm Music

Son, we tried
      to fix

you. Halfway

      up, you
cut out. Starts,

      stops. Notes bent. Lost

music. Warped, you skip
      inside us. Orange

tip. Struck,

      your flame
stains us. We skip

      a breath

and hold you. Grooved
      dark. Unseen

nicks. Sky's black disc,

we spin
between static

    and song. Your flashes

fill, our hands
    starred. Brendan,

a storm is not

    your face. We wait
for lightning

    to be light.

——————— · · · ———————

Stunted Crop

Our bed, a dark
>> garden,

>> his head, a sunflower

too heavy
>> on its stem. Husk we can't

>>> discard, he seeds

>> our fallow field, blooms
into night's uprooting,

>> our voices clipped

>>> like stems in water, *He's*
worse. Yeah I know

he's worse! What else

>> *do you want me*
>>> *to do?* Stalk in the wind

shaking us, *Look up, Brendan. We're right*

45

beside you our questions
        sway with him, which useless

           potion to give, liquid pink

     or white capsule, Keppra,
Topamax, Felbatol.

     When they open

         him, sprinkle his mind
    with light, slice

into the charred core

     will the earth
        let him grow?

Give and Take

A ghost mother
                stands at our front door,

     witch daughter by her side.
               Wind blows

through us.
               Outside each house lit

     with jack-o'-lanterns
                  squinting their triangle

fires. My son is a lion,
               runs in circles screaming

     "Hi hai hi." Grace and I
                  don't go out much. He's too

loud.
               He glows inside

     with ancient women
                  burning. Epilepsy is sacred. Epilepsy

is profane.
                    "Trick

         or treat." I offer
                         the candy bowl. *I have little*

left. Our son can't eat
                    sweets. Grace measures

                              his meals. We
         steady him

         with ketosis. The little witch
                    takes a Starburst. *I can give*

this much.
                    He slows, comes

         to my side, his hand cold
                    as stone. Brendan

                                   is a cathedral, radiant
as Joan of Arc with her visions.

"Can I have another?"

her small hand grabs

at the bowl.

I pull away.

Sorry.

No more.

Exhaust

Soot of wounds. The air burning
        somewhere. Mother's weary voice, *Why can't*
you stay home more for us? I land

        in the middle. A room
of fumes, coming gusts, wheels spinning

        over black. *I play music*
for you. All of us. Charred quiet
        behind shut doors. *To earn*

a living. Father's engine idles, his lips
        against her hair. *Only three weeks.* His whisper

cuffing my ear, *You're the man*
        of the house. I drag out bags
of trash, forget to wash

        dishes. Home
from teaching, she gathers our clothes, neatens

        his scores, heaps steaming rice
on my plate. On the couch, her
        exhales. Remnants

of exhaust. Locked in her studio,

      a half hour stolen to paint. Over the phone

her words to him, *Must you go*

      so far? His plane rising, white trails

across blue. Her brush sweeps

      the dark horizon line. How to care

for her. Vapor disappears, Father shakes

      with turbulence. *I'll be home*

soon. At night

      my breath held, I calm

the winds, store him

      in clouds.

Split

Mother is quiet
        while she wraps your trombone and mutes
in cloth, straps them

        in your black suitcase. Your studio
empty, we both know

        its sting, sharp as the split lip
salting my mouth, the dragon's flapping crepe
        lifting away from me

like your plane. Red flames
        bleeding into clouds, gauze

Mother dipped
        in alcohol. Father, the house silent
of you, I hold in words

        the way she does
when she bandages

        me, mirror showing us
the burn of *nip*—the truth
        of our skin.

Tunnel Visions

Bent coins of words
       spill rusty

from his mouth,
       incomprehensible. *I don't quite remember*

my mother says. Rain sheathing

       tires, I swerve
across lanes, in the rearview see

       his wounded
face. *I want to know more*

       I say. A bloody space

between his teeth. The blank shape
       of every loss,

my mother's past. His topaz eyes. Her sand
       portal. Barrack

windows. Shards and crystals. Knives

of lightning, flashes
of carp. *That's what*

I have she says. Her memories
are dark roads. His lips

flicker, unspoken. We enter

the tunnel, climb
the stone throat

to the eye
of light.

Severance

Hand to the wall,
I turn

and push myself
back. Tomorrow, my son cut

open. If I could change us.
My crawl stroke pulls me through—

the pool's cocoon
brings

Rilke's phrase
and my son's bright scan.

My feet push off
underwater light, I swim

back and forth, return
to his candled dome.

―――――――   · · ·   ―――――――

He's on fire,
the screen tells us.
I touch smooth glass,
the heat sealed
within, right lobe
a smoky moon floating
in his skull's armor.

―――――――   · · ·   ―――――――

Twelve hours
away. Darkness begins

slowly.
Grace packs

his suitcase. I raze
wild clover, smooth

the lawn, lucky
four-leaf

in the rusted
blade. Sky

of water, sun
of fire, I dive in

and out. They could cut
too deep.

——————   · · ·   ——————

5 a.m. quiet, tires slick
with rain. Grace in the back seat
holding him, my hand

steering us. Home
falling away, blinded
by granite and fog. Beyond

the jagged mountain, we break
through mist, pass over
water, cross Golden Gate, he smiles

at blinking spires and Presidio hills
ahead. I know
how hope begins—and then doesn't.

———————   · · ·   ———————

We take off
his clothes, tie

the gown. He just turned five

last month. Sealed
in the white envelope

of the bed, he kicks,

and we sever,
give him up

through steel doors.

———————— · · · ————————

A sliver of dysplasia
removed, the blaring
inside stopped.

For now, it's like a quilt
placed over him.
His head, this new, quiet

room. Fire
cut through fire, the noise
extinguished.

———————— · · · ————————

Stitched lines
in flesh, his road

turns through us.
His arms bound, far

from the wound
that marks his head.

Grace adjusts
the gauze, I hold the cup,

water fills
his throat, her hair black

waves. Our cold
house, his bed

waiting, we'll reach
there

if we begin here.

Brendan's Orange

Far from

    the playground,

she wheeled him.

    Shade

of a tree.

    The sun

an orange.

    His skin

felt cool.

    Hand in

her purse,

    she brought out

orange.

It looked

sweet. A treat

he couldn't taste.

We never

let him.

He tingled,

leaned forward,

touched her

wrist. Juice

on her knife.

His lips

dry. Her sound

     sweet.

You'll like this

     she whispered,

held orange close

     to his mouth.

It shined.

     Dripped.

He reached

     for it.

Discovery

The back of their heads.

My son. His son.

Facedown.

Breath on cement.

*   *   *

I dropped dark stars of cannabis on my son's tongue—to calm his blood.

Grace massaged his back, his spastic left arm.

We told the school aide *Never give him sugar.* She nodded at us.

It can trigger a seizure.

*   *   *

The dad read his son *The Little Prince*, *The Fire Next Time*.

Told him *Come back before dark*.

The mom fixed pancakes. Bought him new shoes.

Keep your hands out of your pockets. Be respectful.

*   *   *

Spiking fever. Our son, so dizzy he drops.

Mouth hitting the ground.

A broken tooth. Dead roots.

Orange slices in his vomit. Did this cause the fall?

He couldn't tell us who fed him the fruit.

If he could speak, he'd point at her.

I didn't do it the aide keeps telling us. We don't believe.

Maybe I gave him a few she confesses later. *He wanted to taste something sweet.*

We had no idea the teacher said. *She must've done it when we weren't looking.*

Grace holds my hand. *We should've known.*

*   *   *

Their boy walking home, cell phone left on his bed.

Bag in his hand, reaching inside.

Red light twisting on his face.

The father holding car keys.

I should've picked him up.

The boy raised his arms.

The cops said it wasn't their fault.

*   *   *

The silence of our sons.

Those who are seized.

We keep asking.

Link

On edge, I stand next to my white friends
        beneath crows perched

on wire—beaks pointed at us, wings
        tucked close as rifles, my feet sensing

the rumble as the buses round

the corner, past houses
behind tall fences, kept lawns. At 13, I haven't gone

through the heart of darkness, natives
        in their own land—seen as evil and faceless

on the shore. I've only read about Rosa Parks

staying up front, Martin Luther King Jr. marching through tear gas
        and growling dogs. Hands

on the fence, we peer through holes, yellow steel
        glimmers, faces tinted behind windows, the new

kids approach. *Integration*

                              the papers call it. Shades blended
            into one paint. All of us

                    marked. My Japanese mother and her black friend Gwen
      wielding brushes, on canvas

                        their pigments drying

into the same tone. Splatter of drops
                              on their overalls. My white dad playing trombone

                                    in lights and smoke, jamming
      with his mixed band. The colors and sounds

                              link us. Leaves kicking up, autumn

            smolders, crackle of rumors and gossip, the portrait painted
too simple: rough outlines

            of them in brick tenements, filled in details of fried chicken
      and Cadillacs booming

            with rap, the last touch, tinges of envy

about their moonwalk
and dunks. My mother's words, *You'll make friends*

with them. See who they are
for yourself. The rustle

of wings, a caw begins, *Just be careful*

who you date. Others might not
understand the feathered flock

rises. My mom looked away from me, *I know*
only too well. On steel posts

birds land, buses pull up

to the curb, we walk toward them, two tight lines
passing each other, divided

by chain links. Some kid says, *They're not*
like us. Gusts of wind, my heart darkens. *How do*

you know? My father's words, *Don't always believe*

what you hear. Glass doors hiss

open, a girl descends

stairs, gold hoops glinting. *Love is not a choice*

my mother told me. *It's just easier to marry*

your own kind. My father's parents opened

the door slowly

to her, at dinner avoided

her eyes, his hand holding hers

under the table. *What is my own kind?* Bus doors

closing, through the fence

of linked diamonds, I breathe

in the girl's citrus scent, her shine

reaching me, notes of a song, harsh

and sweet, my parents' house, riffs of brass

and pungent scent of color

on brushes, hard to capture, even now

        on paper, her skin

I want to touch, afraid

        to, she walks by, looks up,

               and we see.

Capture

after the movie, *Fruitvale Station*

Go back. Through holes of light. Gold bullets. Your daughter laughing,
Racing you down alleyways to the car. Sun spun in her hair.
Atone for weed, cheating. Wipe roads skinned dark. Slice rope from acacia.
Nightsticks whipping air, then landing, gather voices, one refrain,
Three words, *Let me go.* Rise before the shot.

James Byrd

What to hold
> when there's nothing

to hold: your hands
> grasping

air, ankles chained

> to a truck. We must
never look

> away. Face
the unimaginable:

> a road of blood

and dust, asphalt
> shredding

your clothes. Skin
> torn to

the bone. Can we

understand
what took them

here, foot pressed
to the pedal, laughing

or quiet

as they pulled
your weight?

This is just
a poem, the search

for words, witness

to your voice
erased

by the rev
of the engine, severed

from your throat.

Shepard Psalm

after Psalm 23

Prepare for enemies:

Warm your feet
from dirt's grave-cold,

uncover your voice,

the words flying out
like leaves

into gusts of their rage.

Dissolve the fist's stain
on your face

and the rope

around your wrists.
Lie down

in the beaten dark,

near pastures green
and unbruised,

the salt raining down

your blood,
restoring

dusk's ragged edge

to smooth plains
of terracotta slate,

your gold-straw hair

igniting the wick
of pink dawn.

You shall not want.

• • •

Broken

The park below gives us fire, orange leaves
      crackling
over green. I gulped coffee as I drove, Grace held
      the cold cloth

on his head. *I do I do* he babbled
      his mantra. Our mouths chalked, minds chipped
      and torn
away. *He never gets better*
      I said. Her lips tightened, *That doesn't*

help us. Back to our corners. Another night
      in ER. Two bags of fluids
      through our eight-year-old son. A flock sweeps
      over, shadows

the flame, spiking mercury,
      the night cracked
      into ice chips, his skin
paling, seizing
      stopped. *Some couples like us*

      end up broken Grace says, rubs
my back. *Not us* I tell her, my hand

on his chest

as he sleeps. Through

the window, I see

kids swinging

into the sky, gulls rising, wings white

as Brendan's shirt, the silk

of Grace's gown. The long field flickering, she leans

against me, our forms resting with his

in glass. A whole life of

I do

I do.

At the Park

an invisible rope pulls
back his head
and a hand rips
the blue sheet of sky.
At the edge of his
world, I make out
his torn voice:
Papa, my eyes
open
the rest of me
closed.

Blind Nights

Never looking
back. The breakup night

I swerved
down the mountain

drunk, beer foaming

between my legs,
ran the red, laughed

at the cop
who passed me

in the fog. Not remembering

what's dangerous.
My son doesn't

listen to *Stop*, I hold up
my hand. He throws

the remote

but can't throw
a ball. Never thinking

ahead. Going inside
a stranger naked,

bursting stars

of blackout.
I never caught

her name. Does my son know
mine? Or Grace's?

His touch

a light flutter says, *I'm here*
his tightening grip, *I'm scared*

Softer, buddy
I say. *It's ok.* Will

a lover ever touch

him? Will he learn to hug
us back? Grace and I

imagine it happens. So perfect
the night

we made him.

Field

I kneel, roll
        the foam ball slow
across the rug

        to you. Blur
of red seams, white sphere

        of memory. Lights orbit
above green
        fields. Leaves scud

off the mound. Leg kicked
        high, I rocket pitches

into my dad's mitt. *Baseball,*
        father, autumn
words you can't

        say. Just this simple
game. *Catch*

        I repeat. Eyes
wavering, you sit, reach
        out. Circling

world, small
        planet. Past

your hands,
        it keeps
spinning.

'Nam

Through your father's hands
        around the wood bat, we knew
he'd been there. He showed us
        how to hit: *Keep your eyes*

open. Grab it tight. Be braver than the ball.
        The pop of oak against leather,
a club against bone.
        Between swings came a sudden

pause, his vision hidden
        behind mirrored glasses, locked on the dot
in the sky. His flinch
        as the bat made

contact, after a branch snapped,
        an engine shot out—the real weight
unknown, buried somewhere in the canvas bag
        we dragged across the field

after practice, sound of helmets
        and balls rolling in the trunk,
his rearview glance—to know
        it was us.

Target Practice

Derek, I guess your father did it
       to make you tough, strapping you

into catcher's gear, tying your hands

       behind your back
placing you

       behind home plate, trapping you

the way he'd been
       in sights

of Viet Cong rifles.

       On the mound
we stood in single file,

       one by one

dipped our hands into the bucket of balls
       we aimed and fired—

Throw hard your father coached us, *Straight*

    at his face.
I want to say

    I didn't like the clang

of a fastball
    off your wire mask, didn't smile

at his praise, *Nice shot.* None of us

    stopped him
mocking you

    as you wobbled

on balls of your feet
    and he yelled *Throw harder.*

I stood beside him, held it

in, flinched at the smack
of leather against

your chest. Your eyes closed

while he screamed *Don't move,*
keep your head up

his fingers tapping

unfiltered Camels, ash drifting like contrails
of vanishing planes. *The war broke*

his mind my parents said,

'Nam growing less distant
each time you were the target, crouched

against our hurling

fire, your Father raising his hand
for us

to cease, leaning over

you, loosening

    the knot, patting you

on the back

    as you shook out
your hands, tore off your mask,

    and we looked away.

Derek's Father Remembers Saigon

The rustle

    in a thicket

of gingko,

    shadows

waiting between

    trees. Teeth

of the gibbon

    glinting

above, my arm

    around the throat

of a stranger,

    choking words

I don't

      understand.

Rough sand

      of his skin, beads

of rain spilling

      into his black

hair. All

      that follows

us. The warmth

      against me, his struggle,

his body

      foreign, I drag him

to the river.

      In the blood-orange

wash

      of the moon,

I lean over

      the current,

let go.

Gold

The sky's flame
        in my watch,
your right hand grips

        the railing. Far off
boys spring up,

        leap into the deep
end. The sharkness
        of their flips, they splash

and glide, sleek and clear,
        fingertips stretched

to the wall. Their wake ripples,
        touches your feet. Bronze
is my palm

        on your back, gleam
of your face

        above silver
water. On the ledge
        you freeze. We sway,

my hands hover. Gold

    when you step in.

Japan

comes through my childhood of cartoon smoke, slant-eyed
      savages with spears. *The gash*
in my son's brain. Afternoons of Looney Tunes

      wartime reruns. *He's Japanese*
from me. Imperial heathens slash

      through brush, machetes
bowing to the jungle sun,
      blood stain

on a flag's white canvas. *The red*
      on his forehead. At seven years old, I jump

up and down on the couch, clap at Bugs Bunny
      holding a bazooka, pouring gunpowder
into the barrel's black hole. *The smell*

      of his brain burning. Sound cranked
loud, the rat-a-tat-tat cuts

through the sizzle of mackerel
and my hunger for fish
     that Mama calls "saba." *Part Chinese*

from my wife I laugh
     at "Ah So," choppy ching-chong, Bugs

dodging dropped bombs. *The drugs that poison*
     him. Over her cast iron
wok, Mama waits for charred

     lines, for silver skin to sear, then turns the flame
low, seals in heat

     with a glass lid. "Shut that off. It's not
funny." *He just turned seven and can't talk.* Her warning
     whirs through the kitchen fan. *More blood*

on his brow. Moving closer, fixed on Bugs, my back
     to Grandpa's scrolls, his bold strokes

on rice paper, Mama's watercolor sea
        swirling with flame, *It's coming* I am struck by Banzai
through the crazed pilot's buck teeth,

        marvel at blitzkrieg speed, *straight at us* the blur
of paws, *We are in*

        its grip twine Bugs tightens
around sticks of dynamite. *It's hell.*
        Kamikazes wave

the flag and smile
        while dying. *When he falls* I am shaken

by their cries choked in glass,
        cockpits shrouded, red drops squeezed
from the sky *We all go down.*

My Son Loses Teeth Across Time, Space, Race, and War

Wherever I am is war. Miles and miles from Grace. *Don't leave me. Alone*

with him. I run through storms of words

          beneath a sky of glittering teeth. My son

grinds his molars, I block out

          sound. "Traitor." Sand stings

my eyes, the sun darkens my face. "Spy." One eye

          on him. *Where was she?* A tooth

could crack. Disappear. White icicles falling

          into my brain. "Terrorist." His scream strafes

the air. *Don't yell*

so loud. Everywhere I go, I am bound. *You're scaring him.* I dive

into a trench, cover my ears. Strap his helmet, a guard

over his mouth. Eyes

on him. He falls. Blood fire. A necklace

of teeth. Tongues

cut. Through the wall, moaning. *Who was*

I? "Jap." She would know. *I didn't mean*

to. My half-white face tinted

red. Liquor flares. Hairpin triggers. His high

pitch. Morning sirens. Planes steam behind clouds. Dripping faucet

in a stone room. Shiny white pebble, his mouth

bleeding. Stain on linen. My son

on his knees. He'll never know

the pledge. Wounded. Heaving

breath. Voltage that pains, but doesn't

kill. To not know, but to hear

in our cells. "We will hunt you down." A weight

against my temple, I begged to leave. *Will we make it?* Blindfolded. *It's not*

too late. I'll see it coming.

If I wake.

Brendan's Twitter

You would say
rocket man

trees on

fire, skies
in smoke. Blue

will clear. The sun

of your hands
on my back.

The world is

never silent.
You hum,

we turn,

leaves fall
closer. Your garden

grows

words inside.
Forest, touch,

inferno.

Sit under
a tree, birds

will talk.

Your life
is hard

to tell.

My Mother in Tanforan

Horses live here with us
        Mama told me.

Straw scratched
        through, wings hovered

above my nose.

        In the stall
I shuddered

        underfoot: rope cinched
around stomping

        legs, hooves running near. A wash

           *

of noise. There's what
        you think

happened
          and what really

happens. *The horses*

          were gone my sister Tae tells me.
Believe this: as a baby

          I knew
smells of manure. Dirt flaked

          from my hair. Beneath spouts

                    *

I shivered, needles
          of ice poured

on my skin. I sense it: hands
          swaddling me

in coats. A tag

    with our prisoner number
flapping against my face. Whinnies,

    moans behind boards.
Shhh. I kick

    the air. Flies

        *

scatter, people hide, the buzz
    stops. The ground

quiets. *Pretend*
    we're horses. Mama's back, a bent

saddle, I climb

    on. We gallop across mud
through gates, over

fences. A dry
green. I think we are

far away.

Gold and Oak

The deaf hear music
like gold coins

in their stomachs.
My boy is an oak,

receives the wind

of our conversation
catches

scattered leaves
of our words. My father's brass,

my brother's string make

sense to him:
Gold comes out clear

from the slide,
laughter folds inside

the bell's rim, ducks

fly out, wonk and quack
in air. A sound

forest. Oak hums
bright, then

deep. The bow smooths out

the noise
in his head,

brown eyes lit
from inside,

my gilded sapling.

Bird Cries

I miss exits, veer
> through the world
dangerous. Drive

> with earplugs, strain my neck
to check if my little boy

> is all right. At home I wear headphones
to block out
> his squawks. In my own

bird cage. *Shut up* I yell when he breaks
> through. Squeeze his cheeks

hard. Hold him by the shoulders. *Be quiet.* A flock
> of seizures. His fingers claw
into my wrist. He says so

> little. I can't shut him
out. His good arm flaps. Shadows swoop

> down on him. I keep him
from falling, keep him
> from flying. *Some sounds are torture*

my dad says. If my boy is quiet, his friends
        will like him. When he screams, neighbors could think

I'm hitting him. I strain
        to hear the radio, cry
when I drive

        to work. A blackbird can be seen
thirteen ways. I fly to retreats to write

        about him. When I come
back, he is still caged. I shampoo
        his hazel hair, and he soothes me

with coos *Ay ai . . . Nice voice buddy*
        I tell him. He nests quiet

in his wheelchair. *Poor little guy*
        my mother reminds, *so much to say*
and no words. His mind a deep sky

        she believes
he will rise into.

Hai

Look. A bird. Mountain.

The sky so long. Blue is where

you go. To the sun.

Blue Creation

My father spins away from us
        in Seattle, plays didgeridoo in Australia, glows blue
on my atlas globe. Mother brushes blue on canvases,

                stitches our denim wounds, knows the cold

                    without him. Blue is him
            circling, her streaks and swirls, thread in our hems, needle
                and wool, sweaters

    she weaves before winter

blows blue against
        our ribs, stays within. *Circular breathing*
he calls the pockets of air he held

            in his cheeks while he let it out, always

                    · · ·

coming back to me
and my mother, Loren, my brother. Blue the wind,
blue the turns we take

being strong. We hold

each other, link to circle
his absent body, blue as the static of distance, the widening
seam, blue soft as her drying paint, sharp as his ink

on postcards, *compose, Aboriginal, continent*—

claws of *koala*, my knife opening
his air-mailed gift, the boomerang Loren and I throw
into the blue, stitching a line

through the sky between us.

Seven Years after My Son's Birth

Super Bowl helmets crash on screen,
fever scoring over

one hundred, Brendan clenching
his mouth. Halftime ad

of a soldier just returned home, duffel bag

over his shoulder, one arm around his wife, the other
dangling, hand missing, flesh wrapped

over bone. Swatting my hand, Brendan sweeps
the air wildly, knocks over chips

and salsa, rug stained red. *Not again* I blurt out, take

a breath, guide him straight, lower him soft
to the couch. Grace tucks a pillow under

his neck, strokes his forehead. Ice on his skin, he grips
my wrist. The young son

clings to the leg

of his father's fatigues, already knowing
to avoid the phantom

hand. Our son resting near, Grace kneels, scrubs out
spattered red of cubed tomatoes. To the sink

I haul the bucket, wring out

the towel. A flag wilted on the pole, the soldier
and his wife step through the screen door, the son

following. My son will be seven
tomorrow. Rising

to his feet, he staggers

as if shot, collapses in my arms. Grace wheels him
to the car. *Get him*

to Emergency. Lashes fluttering, our son
faraway. *We're almost there.* The father looking

past mortar and smoke

to stars. *Let's celebrate our troops
coming home.* The camera

pans in, the freckled boy shaking with laughter
from the fake punch

of his father's only good

hand. Behind the curtain, the nurse's hand trembles,
misses my boy's vein, then steadies, fills him

with sodium chloride, electrolytes, drip
of anticonvulsants, *Prolonged seizing*

causes brain damage. Machine by his bed whirring

like helicopter blades. Should it have been
smaller, the moon sliver

they once removed from Brendan's brain,
or should it have been bigger, a slab

of granite inscribed with names

of the father's missing platoon? Curled
into himself, he freezes, the fluorescent panel

flickers, a bullet
of light, I sink, soft trench

of his mattress, bring him close, his t-shirt soaked

in sweat. Shoes tight on my feet
keep me awake. *Brendan, come back.* In this parched

room his breath lands, rolls
across my chest. Blown sand, we

lift away.

Son Sutra

Boy of stars, sun inside, fallen without a sob,

Rest against me, bending sunflower, still the flutter,

Ease your head, son, it's late,

No way to before, your skull shadowed and sunlit, turn,

Deepen us with your shadow words, muted son, say *dad*

After me, your scattered sun petals, our sutra

Nightfall, I gather you, my bruised son.

My Mother Watches Horses with Brendan

Through the fence you look out,

    their hooves breaking new earth.

Sleek fur the shade

    of bourbon. Kicking up clods

of green. I wheel you closer

    to shaken ground. Grandson,

at ten years old, you point at them. Once, I thought

    you said the word, *horse*.

Someday I'll paint you

    the story. Topaz rain galloped

over roofs, barracks thundered. We were the ones

corralled. My hands

on your shoulders, your hand taps

my wrist. *Look. They are*

flying. Over crests of hills. Running into

the sky. Go far enough, speak

what you can, there's love

in silence, all things, they come and go.

Da

skips through our house, his

    pebble of sound. Ripples in

the lake of my chest.

Robin

Thump
      against glass,
            a brown feather
falling.
      On its back,
         wing flapping.
In his wheelchair
           my son leaned
      for its song.

       *

He's not normal.
      The jolt
           of diagnosis.
      My hands
         squeezing hard
at the stop sign, trying
         to turn, Grace quiet
beside me. Through the windshield
        misted
    with rain, the street,
           leaves of elms blurred.

*

I punched holes
                        through the cardboard lid
so the bird could breathe
                        and rest
        in dappled shade,
        peck at seeds
                        undisturbed, sip the saucer
of water. At night
                        I shifted
        the lid
                        slightly open, could see it
inside, still breathing,
                                sensing the sky,
                its bent wing
                        spreading out again.

*

He needs us to tie
              his shoes, but he understands so much Grace says. *He lifts*
    his plate when I cook his meals. Touches his glass for water.
                       He's good at opening things
                               I add. *Maybe he'll*
              be a doorman. We always smile
at this. Our eleven-year-old boy chirps and trills
          inside his tented bed,
               calls for us forever
in our nest of blue wood.

*

A flame
       in my hands,
             its red belly
trembled. A chirr
              from its throat, wing
         fluttering.

Brendan poised

        in his chair, legs straining, the robin

    lifted away.

          *

From his seated nest

        he points

   at the steel walker. I pull him

           up, help him

     stand, secure him in, black straps

  striping

         his back. Left arm

     unfolding, right one

          gliding, he circles

the table, squawk filling

        the house. Light falling through

  the window,

      I shadow him

          and he flies.

Brendan's I Am

A close flash,

    quick torrent.

The sounding

    near. It happened

in time. The path

    deepened, water reached

the house. Our son, 14, walked alone

    to his blue stroller chair. Wheels

locked, we strapped

    him in,

his body still

    as Buddha

beneath the tree.

I steadied the bowl.

Grace raised

the spoon

of broth

to his lips. Her words *Brendan,*

we just want you

to have

a happy life.

Silver

touches his tongue.

Two syllables

gush from

his mouth.

Rain

gathers, our eyes close,

the current flows

through us.

His first real

sentence.

I am.

Through

In my granite mask

     I take

off. With sparkles

     of touch

     *   *   *

you stun me

     back. Together, we walk,

soften

     the dirt. Our steps

     *   *   *

crystal footprints, we clear

the path. Through

the glass

earth, we open.

Tangle

Did I poison his seed? He yellowed, a plant needing
        water. All they could do—
shine lights to cure the jaundice. I am

        knotted. Grace's mother, *Give him liquids.*
The doctor, *Hold back so he'll latch on.*
        And my mother's question, *What did you eat*
and drink that night? My veins filled

        with sashimi's mercury, liquid gold Sapporo
in the tatami room where Grace and I made love
        and Brendan began. Outside the *ryokan*

window, Ito's river twisted into the sea,
        my half-Japanese and her full Chinese
fusing into a strain impure and volatile.
        Chromosomes unwed

as we unite. Our double helixes, a strong
        braid that unravels,
toxic. The needle's sting, vaccines

        flow through his veins. Holistic,
megadose miracles. *Tsubo* pinpoints

on his skin. Fragile X
tests. Fecal transplants. We are pulled

too close. Woven together, we might
mend him. My mother *Jin Shin Jyutsu's* him, warm hands
on his cranium. My father crushes vitamins

on his food. *He'll be fine*, Grace's father
says. After hours with him
only one half-built tower. We search surgeons
to take him apart, bring him

back better. One Chinese doctor says, *Each seizure*
shakes the tree within, frees him
from the past. Spirited through

by his ancestors. This tangle could mean I am
a good father. Grace, a good mother. I help him stack
the tower higher, open his trust account.
She steadies him

on the tricycle's black seat. His rhythms
and circles guide, dizzy, disorient us. We follow
jagged lines, come to loose ends, pick up

broken branches. Never just one
        way. The tangle. This could mean
it's all his fault. Or all ours. This could mean
        we'll let go. Or we'll never

have to. A gold knot
        of shadow and light,
he binds us.

Notes

Seize enters an existing discourse and growing body of literature about children with disabilities, special needs, and those who are neurodiverse. In the process of writing this book, I discovered various authors who offered inspiration. Ian Brown's *The Boy in the Moon* and Kenzaburo Oe's *A Healing Family* resonated, spurred me on to keep exploring this challenging, wondrous terrain. Edited collections—Sean Thomas Dougherty's *Alongside We Travel* and Suzanne Kamata's *Love You to Pieces*—provided community. A number of brave writers and poets bring me strength, including David B., Buzz Bissinger, Jennifer Franklin, Edward Hirsch, Rupert Isaacson, Kamilah Aisha Moon, Oliver de la Paz, Connie Post, Emily Rapp, Brenda Shaughnessy, and Timothy Shriver.

"Seized" was based on a prompt from Judy Halebsky in my writer's group, Poet's Choice, about sense of place, which coincided with a poem I was writing for an exhibit in the Thacher Gallery at the University of San Francisco, curated by Glori Simmons. Entitled "In Nature's Temple: Early California Art & Ecology," the exhibit showcased writings by John Muir, paintings by William Keith, and photographs by Carleton Watkins and Eadweard Muybridge. Various images and text served as catalysts for inspiration in the writing of the poem.

"My Mother at One" emerged from a writing exercise from Amy McInnis Norkus of Poet's Choice, in which one chooses ten words from a passage of fiction and integrates them into a poem. My words are drawn from Tim O'Brien's *The Things They Carried*, "Spin," p. 35-40.

Certain words and phrases in "Brendan Lexicon" are drawn from his medical reports.

"Jap" was first inspired by Bob Hicok's "Nigger."

Parts of "Give and Take" are informed by Jon Meacham's article, "A Storm in the Brain," *Newsweek*, April 20, 2009, p. 38-41.

"Capture" is dedicated to the memory of Oscar Grant III (1986-2009) and was inspired by the film, *Fruitvale Station*.

"James Byrd" is dedicated to the memory of James Byrd Jr. (1949-1998).

"Shepard Psalm" is dedicated to the memory of Matthew Shepard (1976-1998). This poem was originally inspired by the powerful film, *The Laramie Project*, and borrows phrases from Psalm 23.

Acknowledgments

The following journals published these poems, some of them in earlier versions and with different titles:

32 Poems, Alaska Quarterly Review, Beloit Poetry Journal, Boulevard, The Cortland Review, Diode, Hyphen, Meridian, Missouri Review, New Ohio Review, North American Review, Post Road, River Styx, Shenandoah, South Dakota Review, Southern Humanities Review, The Southern Review, TriQuarterly, and *Waxwing.*

"'Nam" was reprinted in *Vice-Versa.*

"Give and Take," "A Boy," and "Seized" were nominated by *Beloit Poetry Journal, Shenandoah,* and *Waxwing* for Pushcart Prizes.

"Truce" received a Best of the Net nomination from *TriQuarterly.*

This book emerged from the necessity to understand my special son, Brendan, and my complex emotions as a father. Throughout the process of writing and revision, I have been blessed by the insight of wise guides, power of family and friendship, and strength of community.

Brendan is. His enlightened, pure presence guides us. His powers reach beyond, take us to new places. Grace, my beautiful soulmate, further illuminates our way. Bo, the dog we rescued, in turn, rescues us.

Our families are anchors of strength, our solid foundation. Deepest gratitude to my parents, Stuart and Renko, role models in life and art, and to my brother, Loren, for our unique, unbreakable bond. Grace's parents, Lok and Chi-Ieng, and sister, Candace, radiate unwavering love. I am moved by the ongoing support of the extended Ishida and Dempster families—especially Aunt Tae and cousin Eric for their caring help and companionship; cousins Paul and Rebecca, aunt Nori and uncle Mike, uncle Kaz and aunt Sachi, the late uncle Stan, uncle Doug and cousin Sarah, sister-in-law Margaret and niece Nona for their thoughtfulness and our vital kinship.

My friends and honorary brothers, Dard Neuman, James Tjoa, and Marc Wallis, energize me with meaningful dialogue and keep me in an authentic space. Toru Saito and the late Bessie Masuda always welcomed us and our son into their home. To Brendan's past and present aides, teachers, doctors, nurses, physical, speech, and occupational therapists, and others—we give praise and blessings. For being such an integral part of Brendan's team, I recognize the following people: super caregivers Rachelle McCaslin and Lynn Porter along with Micah Contreras, Ivy Gaerlan, Barrie Nolan, Briana Salazar, Ginny Schneider, Karen Snow, and Susan West; teachers Laura Becker, Kim Cochrane, Wyoming Irwin, Jennifer Madden, Kate Mansour, Erin Muldoon; doctors Martin Ernster, Meghan Gould Nishinaga, Joseph Sullivan; dentists Dr. Doris Lin-Song, Dr. Ralan Wong, and dental assistant Remie Aranda; social worker Wendy Nauman; KEEN director Melissa Rushefski and volunteer Zoe Shulman; Janet Miller and PAASS.

Just as it has taken a village to raise my son, so has this book been the product of community. To my longtime editing partner and honorary sister, Anastasia Royal, I offer heartfelt thanks: for providing insightful edits and valuable suggestions, and helping me realize the work's true vision. A shout out to Anastasia's husband, Hannes Vermeulen, for his kind spirit and support of our collaboration, her sister Dr. Barbara Royal for integrative medicine guidance, and her mother, Charlotte Royal, for sage advice. These poems benefited from helpful comments on the manuscript at various stages by my friends and fellow writing group members of Seventeen Syllables: Jay Ruben Dayrit, Lillian Howan, Caroline Kim-Brown, Grace Loh Prasad, Brynn Saito, and Marianne Villanueva. Domo arigato to Sabina Chen, Roy Kamada, and Grace Talusan for staying connected. A number of poems were inspired by writing prompts from Poet's Choice. Genuine appreciation to Dean Rader for our friendship and to Chris Haven, Aaron Brossiet, Ashley Cardona, Brian Clements, Judy Halebsky, Amorak Huey, W. Todd

Kaneko, Amy McInnis Norkus, Christina Olson, and Jean Prokott for their positive energy and feedback.

Mentors, colleagues, and friends sustained me during this period of writing. My warm thanks go out to Garrett Hongo for his kindness, generosity, and firm belief in my work, and to Richard Tillinghast for camaraderie and our connection. Patrick Phillips is the definition of true friend and perceptive reader. The invaluable encouragement of Li-Young Lee, Rusty Morrison, and J. Allyn Rosser strengthened me. A special nod to Joan Houlihan and the Colrain Poetry Manuscript Conference for critiquing and nurturing the work. My profound appreciation is due to Martha Rhodes for her warmth and editorial insight and to the amazing team at Four Way Books: Sally Ball, Ryan Murphy, Clarissa Long, and Bridget Bell.

For the gift of funding and time to develop the manuscript, I am indebted to various organizations: the San Francisco Arts Commission for an Individual Artist Grant; the Center for Cultural Innovation for an Investing in Artists Grant (Artistic Innovation category); and the University of San Francisco (USF) for a sabbatical. A USF Sabbatical Support Award, Post-Sabbatical Merit Award, and Faculty Development Fund Awards offered crucial support. The journal editors who first published many of these poems fortified my resolve.

The Lotus Sutra—practiced by my late grandfather, Archbishop Nitten Ishida—brought forth flowering from the mud. Pema Chödrön's *When Things Fall Apart* and other spiritual guides and texts kept me on the middle path. And to all those who opened doors for Brendan and us, we send loving gratitude.

Brian Komei Dempster's debut book of poetry, *Topaz* (Four Way Books, 2013), received the 15 Bytes 2014 Book Award in Poetry. His poems have been published widely in journals such as *New England Review, North American Review, Ploughshares,* and *TriQuarterly,* along with various anthologies, including *Language for a New Century: Contemporary Poetry from the Middle East, Asia, and Beyond* (Norton, 2008) and *Asian American Poetry: The Next Generation* (University of Illinois, 2004). He is editor of *From Our Side of the Fence: Growing Up in America's Concentration Camps* (Kearny Street Workshop, 2001), which received a 2007 Nisei Voices Award from the National Japanese American Historical Society, and *Making Home from War: Stories of Japanese American Exile and Resettlement* (Heyday, 2011). His work—as a poet, workshop instructor, and editor— has been recognized by grants from the Arts Foundation of Michigan and the Michigan Council for Arts and Cultural Affairs, the California State Library's California Civil Liberties Publication Education Program, the Center for Cultural Innovation, and the San Francisco Arts Commission. Dempster has also received scholarships to the Bread Loaf Writers' Conference. He is a professor of rhetoric and language at the University of San Francisco, where he serves as Director of Administration for the Master of Arts in Asia Pacific Studies program.

Publication of this book was made possible by grants and donations. We are also grateful to those individuals who participated in our 2019 Build a Book Program. They are:

Anonymous (14), Sally Ball, Vincent Bell, Jan Bender-Zanoni, Laurel Blossom, Adam Bohannon, Lee Briccetti, Jane Martha Brox, Anthony Cappo, Carla & Steven Carlson, Andrea Cohen, Janet S. Crossen, Marjorie Deninger, Patrick Donnelly, Charles Douthat, Morgan Driscoll, Lynn Emanuel, Blas Falconer, Monica Ferrell, Joan Fishbein, Jennifer Franklin, Sarah Freligh, Helen Fremont & Donna Thagard, Ryan George, Panio Gianopoulos, Lauri Grossman, Julia Guez, Naomi Guttman & Jonathan Mead, Steven Haas, Bill & Cam Hardy, Lori Hauser, Bill Holgate, Deming Holleran, Piotr Holysz, Nathaniel Hutner, Elizabeth Jackson, Rebecca Kaiser Gibson, Dorothy Tapper Goldman, Voki Kalfayan, David Lee, Howard Levy, Owen Lewis, Jennifer Litt, Sara London & Dean Albarelli, David Long, Ralph & Mary Ann Lowen, Jacquelyn Malone, Fred Marchant, Donna Masini, Louise Mathias, Catherine McArthur, Nathan McClain, Richard McCormick, Kamilah Aisha Moon, James Moore, Beth Morris, John Murillo & Nicole Sealey, Kimberly Nunes, Rebecca Okrent, Jill Pearlman, Marcia & Chris Pelletiere, Maya Pindyck, Megan Pinto, Barbara Preminger, Kevin Prufer, Martha Rhodes, Paula Rhodes, Silvia Rosales, Linda Safyan, Peter & Jill Schireson, Jason Schneiderman, Roni & Richard Schotter, Jane Scovell, Andrew Seligsohn & Martina Anderson, Soraya Shalforoosh, Julie A. Sheehan, James Snyder & Krista Fragos, Alice St. Claire-Long, Megan Staffel, Marjorie & Lew Tesser, Boris Thomas, Pauline Uchmanowicz, Connie Voisine, Martha Webster & Robert Fuentes, Calvin Wei, Bill Wenthe, Allison Benis White, Michelle Whittaker, Rachel Wolff, and Anton Yakovlev.